In the Element

Earth, Fire, Air, Water, Ether

Gauri Jauhar

BookLeaf
Publishing

India | USA | UK

Dedication

To my mom, who brought in me the love for words and the magic they weave.

To the Elements of Life, that make and sustain life.

Acknowledgements

The Eight Elements by Ranchor Prime.

The author acknowledges her brother, dad, mentors and friends who have encouraged her poetic spirit and love for exploration with the photographic lens.

Preface

In the Element, is a collection of poems devoted to an intimate exploration of the five elements of earth, fire, air, water and ether that make our existence possible.

It celebrates the dance of these five elements through time and space, individually, and together as they unite. The photographs in the book are based on Gauri's travels and some are taken at the time of the pandemic.

Roots

Roots, above ruins
Stand witness to victory, over war
Shelter history, under ruin
In rapture, is the traveller
Of stories, told and untold
Of heroes, sung and unsung
Of what lies underneath it all
A mystery, continuously sensed
Only, partially seen and savoured

Earth, an Accordion

A wave of sound
A balance of motion
A range of the alphabet
Showing the grandeur of melody
All in a moment, of earth's healing vibration

Eternal Rose

What is the rose-mind?
What is the rose-soul?
The labyrinth like rose-body is a mystery
A keeper to a billion hearts and hopes
Where did the lines blur...oh rose-mind,
rose-soul, rose-body?

Trudging the n-th cross road in New York
In a New York minute, a new rose rendition
manifests
The steel-rose invites
To a world of art inside
The rose, standing still in steel
Made by humans
Yet mysterious and magical

Desert Rose

The folds of the Desert Rose
Grace in every turn
Tells a story of minerals and mines
Deepest treasures of the Earth
A rose takes shape in the depths of the magic
of Earth
Bringing the healing of Mother Earth and
Father Sky
Yin with Yang
All in a fold of the Desert Rose

Fire...the final countdown

The wood is ready
Eternal fire waits to light
The onward journey

(This Haiku is inspired by my first visit to the
Dasaswamedh Ghat in Varanasi, seeing the
wood ready to light the funeral pyres. And, I
would like to share the words of a yogi Guru
Singh, "Death is only a death of the five senses
and the five elements, not of the being")

Rays of hope

Meditative dawn
Inspiring awe around all
Where will this light lead?

The Golden Hour

A meditative dawn at Periyar
A morning glow on Grand Canyon
A crimson glow silhouettes a boat on Malacca
Straits
Far later, Ever more
Hope nestles in a pandemic sunrise over a
tomb
Mystic Mount Fuji, amidst first rays of sun
and clouds
A sky that brings me in prayer
The sky that speaks to you, just to you
As the heart yearns for another sunrise,
another sunset

And it opens the portal of promise, and
dreams
Nature's paintbrush on the longest way
around, to the shortest way home, on an inner
journey

Igniting...Agni

Transitions, to transform
Breathing into the fire that stokes
The crackling heat, when it begins
A warmth of the flame of bonhomie
And then, a calm coolness descends of
making it through
Where there is smoke, a fire burns
Where there is fire, being transforms the
doing

Air, of new possibilities

Veil lifts to the blue
Flights of fancy open up
Breathe joy of degrees

Peace, in the Air

A willow chair sees
For new stories of peace told
To the tree of life

Light and clouds in air
Tulip blooms delight the sky
Splendour of colour

Purity, en Air

This air is pure rare
Plumes of divinity
Grace of mother earth

Magnanimous air
In its healing embrace shines
Speaks of a rainbow

Mystic Dance of Lights

There was the air of music in the mood up above
The taste of hot chocolate and mulled wine warmed the soul, so deep
Ready for a mystic dance of light in the skies
The Igloos, dressed in white, ready for the night of a lifetime
When the skies did an ecstatic dance
Tip-toeing to the soul's beat
Northern lights, full with pixie dust

A rarefied feeling

With bated breath for the majestic,
Himalayas
Is this the foremost one?
The metaphor of a lifetime, The Everest
As I see it, I am ready to set forth
To old mountains, new mountains
The jubilation bubbles, at its magnificence
And, I, take repose in the union of heaven
and earth
Ever present, Ever intriguing, Forever in
reverence

Monsoons

When will monsoon, landfall?
Tracing rain form sky
Petrichor-rich memories
Farmers and romantics, on edge
Rhythm of mausam flows
Tempring singe of summer
Bounties of earth sprout
Colours of romance spring
Tin roofs sing to the soul

Music of drop, after, drop
Malhars serenade skies
Join to shine the sun bright, clear pasts
With rainbows, waiting in the wings

Emerald waters

Wide emerald views
Of a lightness of being
Reaching, far and near

This is it

Tears welled up, where words couldn't
Touched by the subtle folds of, flow
The body I once knew, and revered, was in
ashes
The gentle flow embraced, the spirit
Sun shining bright on the ripples of life
The heart not knowing where to turn
But to accept
This is the defining moment
This is the final countdown
The last breath, as it rests on the flow of life
A new spell of mystery

Deep reverence for the holy Ganges
Somehow, somewhere the faces that once
were...live on
Recharged, in spirit
I return
The journey continues

Flow

With the rhythm of breath
In the pulse of time
Past, present, future
All in the shimmer of, life in a span of a
moment
A river of memories
A stillness in the drop of a moment, now
Ready for an ocean of possibility
How will it unfold?
A mystery to behold
Living all four seasons
Through the sands of time
To all the ebbs and flow of the tide
The potential of a new moon

The grace of a full moon
A fullness in flow of beauty
A deep, meditative, silence in the soul

Imagine

Imagine, the storm in the teacup settles
Imagine, the rustling leaves of fall dance to
the rhythm
Imagine, the snow touches the silence in the
soul
There is peace in the air
There is a movement of love
It's in the, here and now
It's in the, infinite eternal

Sacred Geometry

The balance of life force spins
The kundalini energy rises
Chakra, after chakra, opens like a lotus
The fiery red grounds, base up
The orange orb creates, and astonishes
The luminous sun, transforms
The royal green heart, opens and loves
The deep blue, reveals an inner truth
While the instinct of a deeper blue smiles in
an inner knowing
...that the violet of the thousand petalled
lotus, reigns in pure white

Transformation

The turn of the seasons
Of trees, and life
The passing of clouds
To bluer skies of clarity
The unfurling of the wings of the butterfly
An igniting idea rising from roots to records
Manifesting dreams
Liberating ideas
Transitions, turning to transformations
Flowing with the gentle waves
Braving the storms
To find a new shore, and rest
Till the cycle of exploration continues

Je ne sais quoi

A dance of elements
A dance of colours
Comfort of consciousness
Seeping deep within
The light of this moment, in its fullness is the
truth
Knowing still, the sands of time are slipping
An inner smile, radiates outwards
The heart has its reasons
As it sees the moon move across the skies
What phase does the moon, foretell?
Metta moments, meet with grace
With angels aboard, in caravans of peace

Mahakumbh

A spiritual odyssey
Undertaken to reach, the farthest reaches of
the soul
What is in grasp, what is in reach?
Do the feet know the soul's beat?
Trust in the universe springs eternal like hope
Fears melt in the waters of faith
A unity in humanity emerges from the depths
of the earth
Seeing strangers as friends in faith

Feeling no distance in the vast spiritual space
of the horizon
With gentle feet and touch the journey back
feels haloed
A glow of purpose and spirit

www.ingramcontent.com/pod-product-compliance
Lightning Source LLC
Chambersburg PA
CBHW050750180726
48003CB00020B/2319